GETTING STARTED IN
CANDLEMAKING

Walter E. Schutz

GETTING STARTED IN
CANDLEMAKING

Collier Books, New York, New York
Collier-Macmillan Ltd., London

BOOKS IN THE *GETTING STARTED SERIES*

African Crafts
Batik
Candlemaking
Ceramics
Dried Flower Craft
Egg Decoration
Handmade Rugs
Kitemaking
Leathercraft
Mineral Collecting
Plastics
Prints and Patterns

Copyright © 1972 by The Macmillan Company

All rights reserved. No part of this book may be
reproduced or transmitted in any form or by any means,
electronic or mechanical, including photocopying,
recording or by any information storage and retrieval
system, without permission in writing from the Publisher.

The Macmillan Company
866 Third Avenue, New York, N.Y. 10022
Collier-Macmillan Canada Ltd., Toronto, Ontario

Library of Congress Catalog Card Number: 70–183410

First Collier Books Edition 1972

Printed in the United States of America

Contents

Foreword

If this book is successful in teaching the fundamentals of candle-making, I must thank my wife Sophie, for it was she who suggested that I gather together all the data accumulated during my years of candlemaking and write a book about it.

Thanks also goes to my editor, Susan C. Shipman, who liked the idea and the outline I presented to her.

In preparing this book we first had to try every known method of candlemaking, improving on old practices and developing many new ones of our own. This meant pouring candle after candle until we were satisfied that each procedure outlined here is the best one possible. Then we had to photograph all the finished candles and all the processes for the instructions. Our friend Bernard Hagedorn, of Sister Bay, Wisconsin, helped in this area by taking the color pictures which add so much to the book; to him we extend sincere thanks.

Next we wrote and rewrote the instructions to make them as clear and simple as possible.

Our final task was to weave all of this work into an acceptable manuscript. For the typing of it we owe thanks to Ann Young, who took the time necessary to do it from her busy Island schedule.

We hope we have succeeded in what we set out to do, and that you will share our enjoyment in the absorbing hobby of candle-making.

Walter E. Schutz
Washington Island, Wisconsin

Introduction

The flickering flame of a candle is a kind of tranquilizer. If you watch it in a darkened room, a great sense of peace and calm comes over you, and cares and problems are momentarily forgotten. This quieting effect, in such contrast to the hustle and bustle that normally surrounds us, is undoubtedly the reason why candles are so popular today.

Dining by candlelight, either at home or in a restaurant, is ever so much more enjoyable than eating under the harsh glare of electric bulbs. Everything seems to quiet down; even voices are subconsciously hushed. In the living room, candlelight imparts graciousness, elegance, and intimate charm, thus adding glamour to many an otherwise ordinary occasion.

Just as styles and tastes change in everything associated with our everyday living, however, so too do candle styles. Until a short time ago the "frilly" style candle was the "in" thing. The more flowers, glitter, and gaudy-colored spray paint that were used, the more beautiful the candle was considered to be. Today an earthy style is more acceptable. Bright pinks and pale pastel tints have been replaced by browns, natural greens, oranges, and yellows. Shapes have also changed, as a stroll through any candle shop in your city will reveal. The long, slim taper that was most popular in the past has given way to the bold, squatty, block-type candle.

Because of these changing interests, we have not included in the book the old-fashioned, slim taper candle or those decorated with glitter and flowers. Instead you will find styles, shapes, and colors that fit in best with modern-day living. The shapes are bold and the colors are restrained.

Just as there are many candle styles, so are there many ways to pour and cast candles. Some of the more advanced methods will not be explained in detail, however. These include the use of molds that can be made with latex rubber, a material that enables you to take any figure and duplicate it in exact detail; with one well-made rubber mold, dozens of duplicate candles can be produced. Another method, perhaps the latest development in candlemaking, employs sand for the mold, producing free-form candles in hundreds of different shapes and designs.

Free forms are also made of aluminum foil. Then there are the wild conformations, generally known as "fantasy" candles, that are made by immersing liquid wax in cold water and used to tell fortunes. There are many more ways of making candles, and once you have learned the techniques involved in making basic poured candles, you can try some of these advanced procedures or even try dipping candles. This is a method in which the wick is dipped repeatedly into melted wax so that the body of the candle increases with each immersion. Since dipping is an entirely different way of making candles and has no direct bearing on the molded, or cast, way of producing them, it has not been treated here.

Hopefully this book on candlemaking will give you the help and inspiration you need to make beautiful, practical candles for your own use and for gifts. You should have no problems with any candle you undertake because the instructions are clear and well-illustrated, and the author has tested and retested every operation to be sure that each procedure will be successful.

You are probably impatient to pour a candle as quickly as possible, but it would be a mistake to plunge right in without first reading the entire book, especially the first seven chapters, so that you have a general idea of what the hobby is all about. Also, you will progress faster and farther if you limit your first attempts in candlemaking to the simpler candles. Do not try to make the most ornate or difficult one shown in this book and do not try to duplicate those you have seen in stores. By making very simple ones first, you learn as you go along, avoiding failures and saving materials. First pour a simple candle like the one shown in Figure 19. Then try coloring. Add a simple decoration, using some old braid or a few pine cones or leaves and see how the candle improves. Next try a little bigger candle, perhaps a square one that offers more area for decoration. Experiment with more colors, and try making candles such as those shown in

Figure 26, and Plate 3, on which the decoration is just an easily applied decal. Or shape the outside with a hot knife or wood-burning pen as shown in Figure 32.

In every operation you will acquire new skills. As you progress you will become more proficient and your products will take on a beauty and character all their own. The experience you gain will dictate which candle to try next, and sooner or later you will try to make every candle shown here. But don't limit yourself to mere imitation. Take the instructions for one candle and apply them to another—there is no limit to the different effects you can achieve.

Candlemaking is an exciting art form. It stretches the imagination and the results are always satisfying. It's fun to convert a slab or box of paraffin into a practical object of beauty. It even opens a way for you to make extra money for yourself, since you will find many people eager to buy your finished candles.

There is yet another plus for candlemaking. With almost any other hobby, failure means a loss of materials. Not so with candlemaking. No matter how poorly a candle turns out, there is never any loss of materials. All you need do is remelt the wax and start again. Even the leftover scraps can be utilized, and since the materials cost so little you are not investing a great deal of money.

Follow the instructions and suggestions, and in a very short time you will be producing candles that are every bit as beautiful and professional-looking as the ones you see in the shops.

1

History of the Candle

Ancient man's discovery of fire solved many of his problems. It provided heat for his damp caves, light enough to erase the fearsome darkness and to keep animals away, and even a method of food preparation. In short, the flame opened a whole new way of life for primitive man.

It was probably while he was taking a burning branch or twig from the communal fire that he realized he could transport the heat and light of the fire to the farthest reaches of the cavern in the form of a torch. Possibly, too, he noted that some wood burned brighter and longer than others, and that the stick on which he roasted his meat burned especially bright. When it occurred to him that it was the tallow and fat left by the meat that caused this brightly burning flame, it did not take him long to improve on this method of illumination. Sticks with flaming wads of tallow were stuck into cracks inside the caves and the whole interior was lit up. Since this light kept prowling, hungry beasts away, it is not difficult to see why its apparent magical power was soon transferred to other ways of warding off evils. Consequently fire and the portable flame, and later even the candle, were assigned supernatural powers and accorded much superstitious reverence.

Through the ages, the burning stick was constantly improved

upon. Experience showed that straight-grained wood such as pine, that had a high resin content, burned most consistently. "Splinter" lights made of pine were therefore used throughout all of northern and central Europe, and until recent times, were still popular in some remote Russian villages.

Records show that in ancient Egypt a similar torch or light was further improved by using straight stalks with large pith centers dipped in fat or grease. Perhaps these early torches were the forerunners of the modern candle, since the pith center acted as a wick. The Egyptian development was handed down through the Phoenicians to the Greeks and finally to the Romans, who perfected the entire idea.

The Roman candle took two specific forms. One, similar to a torch, had a predominant fibrous center and was used as a portable light for night travelers. The other had a twisted center core of thin fibrous material such as papyrus or other plant material, and this served as a stationary light inside homes and temples. The torches usually burned fat and grease, whereas the candle, or stationary light, burned liquid tallow or, more often, beeswax.

During the fourteenth and fifteenth centuries candlemakers' guilds were formed in northern Europe. They consisted of two groups: those who made only tallow candles and those who made only wax candles. (The candles used in the churches were usually made by priests, and their production was accompanied by religious rituals.) The men of the candle guilds traveled from town to town and from house to house, making candles for homeowners. These guilds later developed into separate and distinct trade unions. In England the Charter of the Worshipful Company of Waxchandlers dates back to 1484, the guild having started in 1358. The Tallowchandler's Charter is dated 1462.

Candles were most widely used during the eighteenth century, when they were found in all the better-class homes. Prior to this time, candles for household use were made only of tallow. Candles made of beeswax were reserved for church and ceremonial use.

The first big improvement in candle production came with the opening of the whaling industry in the eighteenth century. A crystalline waxy material called spermaceti, that came from the head of the whale, was found to be an excellent material for making candles burn brighter and longer. It is interesting that we still occasionally measure an amount of light by "foot candles." One candle power is the light emitted by a pure spermaceti candle weighing one-sixth pound, burning at the rate of 120 grains per hour.

The next important development in candle production came in 1832 with the discovery of stearin, a material made of both animal and vegetable fats such as palm oil (palmitin) from which the smoky and unpleasant odor of glycerine has been extracted. It is a soft, opaque, white substance which keeps the candle from guttering and adds the strength needed to resist high summer temperatures.

Perhaps the most significant step in the whole history of candlemaking was taken in the middle of the nineteenth century when a revolutionary new material called paraffin was discovered. Made of coal oil, it was produced on a commercial basis by James Young of Derbyshire, England. Almost everyone is familiar with paraffin, since it is available at stores and markets throughout the country. Ideal for candlemaking, paraffin is the basic material in most candles made today. It is used for pouring all the candles in this book. Paraffin produces a highly intense light, but pure paraffin candles are apt to bend during warm weather. To overcome this defect, a mixture of stearin and a small amount of beeswax is added to make a candle with excellent burning qualities. Many other materials such as bayberry wax are used in candlemaking, but since they are not within the realm of the beginner's needs, they will not be covered here.

This brief history of the candle merely touches on the ways in which man has used light through the centuries to further his activities and to improve his life. Familiarity with the development of the methods in which the rushlight, the torch, and the candle were used and held in position frequently leads to the absorbing study of candleholders, candlesticks, sconces, candelabra, and other devices too numerous to list. It also opens the doors to the study of how candles were used in religious rites and ceremonies. If you too decide to pursue these parallel fields of interest, you will find that they will give you many hours of relaxation and add much to your knowledge of this interesting subject.

2

Materials,
Equipment, and
Safety Precautions

Work Area

Most home candlecrafters use the kitchen for a work area (Figure 1). It is convenient because it has heating units for melting the wax, and hot and cold water for heating and chilling the molds. The kitchen is usually a light, airy, and pleasant place to work as well. If a suitable place in the basement or an out-of-the-way room is available, take advantage of the space. Since you need not clean up and put away all of the candlemaking paraphernalia in such an area, you can keep it all handy. With such a setup, you can conveniently make a candle or two even if you have only a small amount of extra time, something you perhaps would not do if you first had to arrange all the necessary materials.

Some candlecrafters build small workshops just for candlemaking, with built-in shelves, bins for wax, and workbenches for pouring and decorating. These workshops can be located in a small corner

Figure 1: Typical kitchen setup for pouring candles.

of the basement, the garage, or in some off-room. The only disad-vantage of the garage is that it is usually not heated during the colder months when most candlecrafting is done. As you become more and more enthusiastic about candlemaking, you might begin to look around for an area reserved for this purpose alone, for you will get much more out of this absorbing hobby if you can set up shop for yourself.

No matter where you work, it is a good idea to protect the area against spilled wax. It seems that no matter how careful one is, there is always the chance that a mold will leak, spilling wax over the table, the floor, and everything else in its way. It is advisable, therefore, to cover the entire floor of the working area with four or five layers of newspaper. If you work on the kitchen table, cover that also. In this way, if you have a spill it is a simple matter to remove the paper and the wax, and the floor and table will have been protected. Instead of newspaper, you can cut old cartons apart and flatten them out to make a mat on which to stand.

Materials

Some hobbies require a long list of supplies or involve the purchase of sizeable and expensive pieces of equipment. This is not the case with candlecrafting. Right now you probably have in your home all the necessary materials and equipment to make a candle. It may not be an elaborate candle of intricate design, shape, and appearance; but you can nevertheless produce a beautiful candle which will be fun to make and which will burn for hours.

Although you can make a candle in a few minutes, using only canning paraffin, a cup or tapered glass for a mold, and a piece of heavy string, it is useful to have a list of the basic materials you will need later on as you get more adept at candlemaking. With the exception of the commercial metal molds, all of the following items are very inexpensive.

BASIC MATERIALS

You will undoubtedly have many of these basic materials on hand already; the others you can easily obtain at local stores:

Newspapers are used to cover the table and the floor of the work area.

Household paraffin, such as that used for canning, is available at your food market. You can also get it in larger quantities from a local oil company or petroleum products firm such as Standard Oil or Shell.

Molds may be adapted from quart, two-quart, or pint milk cartons or any other food containers of tin, cardboard, or plastic. Fancy glasses, cups, vases, and other shapes can also be used so long as they are tapered enough to allow the finished candle to release easily.

Wicks can be made from heavy store string, but standard wicking, obtainable from any of the supply houses listed on page 94, is much more satisfactory.

A double boiler, of the common kind used in the kitchen, is perfectly suitable for melting wax. If it has a pouring spout, so much the better. If you don't have a double boiler, make one by using a deep saucepan with a smaller utensil inside in which to melt the wax or paraffin. Use a trivet to keep the inner utensil away from the bottom of the larger utensil and hence from direct heat.

Heating plate. Use either the burners on your gas or electric stove or a portable electric hot plate. If you plan to purchase a hot plate especially for candlemaking, try to get one with two burners or coils; this will make it more convenient to melt several waxes at a time.

Miscellaneous tools that you have around the house are also necessary. These include scissors, gloves, ice pick or coat-hanger wire, screwdriver, hammer, candy thermometer, spatula, pocketknife, peanut oil, old nylon stockings, and cotton swabs.

Coloring material. You will undoubtedly have a box of old crayons which are excellent for coloring melted wax. If you need more, they are readily available at low cost in almost any store.

With these simple tools and accessories you can pour candles in dozens and dozens of shapes and designs.

ADVANCED MATERIALS

When you become more adept at making candles and have mastered the basic techniques, you will want to try more sophisticated methods of producing and decorating them. Here, therefore, is a list of the materials you can add to your shop for greater enjoyment and production. All are readily available at local stores or candle supply houses.

Stearic acid (stearin) is used to make candle wax opaque and also to promote more even burning of the wax.

Beeswax makes the candles burn more slowly and adds a pleasant aroma.

Wicks of various sizes are available (see page 23), some with a metal core, for the different types and sizes of candles.

Coloring. Although drawing crayons work quite well, color chips made especially for candles produce even brighter colors (see Chapter 7).

Fragrances such as spice, bayberry, cinnamon, and many others, add much to the charm of a candle (see Chapter 8).

Commercial metal molds are not too expensive and they allow you to make candles in different shapes: squares, hexagons, stars, triangles, etc.

Rubber, plastic, and metal molds. There seems to be no end to the shapes available in these molds (see Chapter 4).

Mold or silicone spray is a household product that helps release the hardened candle from the mold.

Decorations. Sequins, glitter, bronzing powders, foil cutouts, paint, artificial flowers, acorns, natural seeds, pine cones, nuts, etc., can all be used as surface decorations. Or they can be embedded into the candle itself (see Chapter 9).

A water bath is a deep container—a pail or plastic wastebasket, for example—used to hold warm water in which molds are placed after the wax has been poured.

A thin sheet wax setup (Figure 56), made of cookie and pie tins placed over an electric fry pan, is used to pour sheets of wax for surface decoration and to keep them soft. The thin wax is often appliquéd to candle surfaces as decoration (see Chapter 9).

Cookie cut-out forms, both in regular and in miniature sizes, are excellent for stamping decorations from thin wax sheeting for surface decoration.

Sculpturing tools such as an electric wood-burning pen, clay sculpturing tools, and such items as large nails, screws, bolts, punches, and tubes are heated and used for sculpturing candle surfaces (see Chapter 9).

Egg beater and fork are useful for making froth wax or snow wax.

Mold sealer keeps wax from leaking out of the mold.

A candle cradle, made of three pieces of wood with padded concave ends to protect candle surfaces (Figure 2), is used when decorating or sculpturing candles. Also shown in Figure 2 is a *swab* of cotton glued to a thin dowel for oiling the inside of a mold.

Tool-heating lamp. This is a handy accessory to have, and as Figure 3 shows, it is relatively simple to make. It has many uses, including the heating of tools used in sculpturing candle surfaces. Any small glass jar with a metal cover will do. Drill or cut a hole in the cover large enough to insert the small piece of ⅜-inch copper tubing. Also drill a small vent hole in the cover to allow air to enter as the alcohol is used up. Solder the copper tube to the cover. The wick is made of ordinary store string.

If you do not want an alcohol lamp such as this one, you can use a candle to heat the tools; however, the soot from the candle flame will dirty the tools and they, in turn, may smudge the wax in the candle. Sometimes this effect adds charm to the finished candle, but you should be aware that such an effect is possible so that it is not incorporated into the candle accidentally.

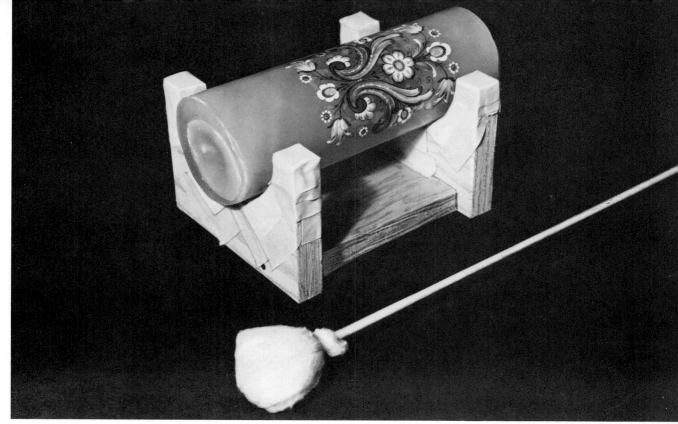

Figure 2: A padded cradle, useful when decorating candles, and a cotton swab for oiling the inside of molds.

Anyone who has assembled all of these tools and accessories can make candles of any shape, color, and description. There is virtually no limit to the possibilities.

Safety Precautions

Paraffin candle wax is as safe to work with as ordinary cooking oil. Neither product is dangerous if handled properly. Wax will not boil,

Figure 3: Tool-heating lamp.

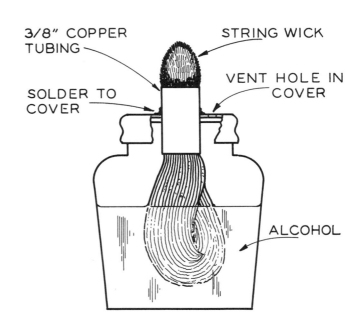

but it will burn. It will begin to smoke and lose color at 250 degrees and it will ignite at 450 degrees. Since the wax need not be heated beyond 200 degrees for candlemaking, it is perfectly safe. It is a wise idea, however, to have a kitchen or candymaking thermometer on hand so that the temperature of the wax can be checked. If you have one, use it; if not, they are very inexpensive and you can buy one at most stores that handle kitchenware.

Hot wax can cause burns on the skin just as cooking oil can. If hot wax spills, apply cold water to harden the wax so that it can be removed; then treat the affected area as you would for any other type of burn, with Unguentine or a similar ointment.

One further word of precaution: be sure to keep hot wax out of the reach of children. In fact, try to keep small children out of the area while you are working. Their boundless curiosity will inevitably tempt them to get in your way.

Before beginning work gather all the necessary materials and place them on the table. Plan ahead, for when the wax is ready to pour, you do not want to have to run all over the house looking for some missing item. Also, it is a good idea to wear heavy gloves that will protect your hands and allow you to pick up a fairly hot mold comfortably.

MELTING WAX SAFELY

NEVER melt wax directly over an open flame or heating coil. Always melt it in a double boiler. As explained previously on page 16, this can be the usual kitchen appliance or one you devise yourself. Don't leave melting wax unattended at any time. *Watch it constantly.*

IN CASE OF FIRE

The best way to snuff out a wax fire is to use a metal cover that fits tightly over the melting container. Have this cover on hand at all times and if the wax should catch fire, place the cover on the utensil and the fire will go out immediately. Do not move the utensil until it has cooled and do not remove the cover. Do not put water on burning wax since this only spreads the fire. Baking soda poured on the fire will help to extinguish it. And it is a good idea to know where your fire extinguisher is so that you can get to it quickly, if necessary.

The foregoing may sound ominous but the same precautions should be taken when heating cooking oil, or when heating and melting paraffin for canning.

3

Candle Wax and Wicks

Wax

The finished quality of your candles depends almost entirely on the quality of the wax used. As already mentioned, the basic material for making candles today is paraffin, a byproduct of the petroleum industry; so throughout this book, the word "wax" should be interpreted as being synonymous with paraffin, unless otherwise stated. Most supply houses have their own brand of candle wax, but you may find that wax from a petroleum company has a lower melting point than you want. (Wax that has a melting point of 143 to 150 degrees is best for candlemaking, and it releases easily from the mold.) For this reason it is advisable for the beginner to start with the ordinary type of paraffin found on store shelves. The finished candle will not be perfect, but you will know immediately if candlecrafting is the hobby for you. You can always get a better grade of wax later.

If you have to order wax by mail from supply houses, one disadvantage is that wax is quite heavy, and the shipping charges are therefore high. On the other hand, in many cities Standard Oil, Texaco, Shell, and other petroleum companies have local branches where they handle this wax, and you can get it from them in any quantity you need. Some have the wax in 50-pound cartons, and although this seems like a large quantity, you will be surprised at how quickly it can be used up in making beautiful candles.

The usual supply-house wax comes in 10-pound slabs. To break a slab into smaller pieces for faster melting, place it in a heavy sack (an old pillowcase or a cloth bag will do) and hit it with a hammer. The bag keeps the wax from scattering around. You can also use a heavy screwdriver and hammer to break large bars into smaller pieces, but some of the wax pieces may fly about.

Since the slabs are 10 pounds each, you can estimate quite accurately the amount needed for a candle. As a general rule, 2 pounds of solid wax are equivalent to 1 quart of liquid wax. Many candlecrafters mark the inside of the melting container at various levels, and instead of weighing the wax, they measure it in liquid form. A 1-quart milk carton uses 1¾ pounds of wax, while a 12-ounce orange-juice can takes about 11 ounces.

To improve the quality of the wax, add stearic acid, or stearin (see pages 13 and 17) which has a melting point of from 122 to 156 degrees. This addition of stearin will assure better molding with greater detail, add strength, and keep the finished candle from bending. All in all it makes a candle burn with a more even flame. The fact that it makes the wax opaque is one of its greatest assets. When stearin alone is added to the wax, it makes the candle white. When added with coloring, it seems to make the colors more brilliant.

Stearin should be used in a ratio of 3 tablespoons to 1 pound of wax. Some candlecrafters use as much as ⅓ stearin to ⅔ wax, but this is a bit high. It is best to experiment and arrive at the proportion that is most suitable for your needs. There are no hard and fast rules, so develop your own formula.

Beeswax may also be used in poured candles. Added to the paraffin and stearin, it will produce a more beautiful and smoother finish on the candle. The addition of beeswax also makes the candle burn slower and minimizes dripping. It adds a golden color to the candle and sends out a nice wax fragrance when the candle is lit. Its only drawback is that it may tend to make the finished candle stick in the mold.

After you have made a number of candles of different wax proportions, you will be able to determine how best to combine paraffin, stearin, and beeswax in order to produce what is usually called molding wax that will be the same as that offered by candle supply houses.

To establish your own formula, perform a series of tests by making small candles that will not take too much wax or require too much time. A candle 1½ inches in diameter and 4 to 5 inches high is about the correct size for these experiments. Use the copper-tube mold described on page 28 (Figure 6) and start with plain paraffin wax. Then add stearin in increased amounts for each successive candle, taking note of the results. Repeat this procedure, adding beeswax to each candle. In this way you will see what results suit you best. There are dozens of other waxes that can be used in candlemaking, but for the beginner this molding wax is the simplest and the least expensive.

Wicks

The wick is the "elevator" of the candle since it brings the melted wax up from the candle to be burned by the flame. Selecting the proper wick is very important because the success of the candle is dependent on it.

As a general rule, the larger the diameter of the candle, the heavier the wick should be. If the wick is too big, too much heat will be generated by the large flame and a hole will be melted on the side. The candle will drip and be ruined. On the other hand, too small a wick will not produce a large enough flame, with the result that the melted wax will not be consumed quickly enough and the flame will get smaller and smaller until it is drowned in melted wax.

One of the biggest candle supply houses recommends *flat braided wicking* of 30 ply for candles 2 inches or more in diameter, and *square braided wicking* for candles less than 2 inches in diameter. You may find other listings, such as *fine*, for candles up to 1 inch diameter; *medium* for 1 to 1½ inch diameter; and *heavy* for any size over 2 inches.

Metal-core wicking is used when you pour a candle into a solid mold—a fancy glass, for instance—in which there is no way to hold the regular braided wicks in place. This wicking has a metal core, usually a very fine lead or magnesium wire, around which the wick is woven. The core makes the wick rigid, enabling it to stand in place without any extra support (Figure 49). It is supplied in *small* for container candles under 2 inches in diameter, *large* for candles 2 to 4 inches in diameter, and *extra large* for candles over 4 inches in diameter. When using metal-core wicks, it is a good idea to wax the end of the wick to facilitate burning for the first time.

Homemade wicks are easy to make, although this seems unnecessary in view of the fact that the cost of manufactured wicking is so low. In addition, it is difficult to control the size of the string used in homemade wicks, and as a result burning is often uneven and sputtery. If you do decide to make your own wicks, however, keep in mind that ordinary thin store string is much too light to serve as a wick, and therefore it should be twisted double. This will produce a *small* wick. The heavy white cotton string usually used to tie postal bundles may be used for *heavy* wicking. With some giant candles (8 inches to a foot in diameter) you can use regular braided clothesline for a wick. Again, you will have to experiment before deciding on the wick best suited for the candles you make.

In making your own wicks, be sure to use only white cotton fiber string. The heavy brown string made of jute will not absorb the melted wax.

To improve the quality of homemade wicks, allow the string as well as the clothesline, to soak for at least 12 hours in a solution of 2 tablespoons of common table salt and 4 tablespoons of borax. Allow to dry before using.

For insertion of wicks, see pages 39–41.

4

Candle Molds

It is generally true that almost any container that will hold a liquid can be used as a candle mold. The only restriction is that its sides must be at least straight, although it is better to have them slanted and tapered so that the finished candle can be released easily. Needless to say, the sides should have no embossed parts which would hinder the release of the candle.

Types of Molds

There are various types of molds: homemade molds, commercial molds manufactured by candle supply houses, ceramic molds usually used to cast plaster of paris figurines, and many other more advanced kinds.

Homemade paper molds are made from a wide variety of materials (Figure 4): paper milk cartons, ice-cream cartons, cheese-dip cartons, orange-juice cans, or any similar container. Many of these are wax-coated and can be used without any further treatment, although it is always a good idea to give all molds a spray of silicone, candle-release spray, or kitchen oil. Other paper boxes and forms such as oatmeal boxes, breakfast-cereal

Figure 4: Cartons and forms used as molds in candlemaking.

boxes, prune boxes, and paper mailing tubes may also be used, but with these it is imperative that they be given a heavy coating of mold release or silicone spray, since the cardboard would otherwise absorb some of the wax and the candle would not release easily. In addition the surface of the candle would not be smooth.

Figure 5: Candles made from paper-carton and cup molds.

Orange-juice cans with peel-off tops are really paper, even though they look like metal. They make splendid molds for the short, stubby candles that are currently so popular (Figure 50). To use them, remove the peel-off top from each can, cut off the remaining top edge, and give the can a coat of silicone or candle-release spray. Candles made in homemade paper-carton and cup molds are shown in Figure 5.

Wicks can be inserted after the wax has been poured by using a heated ice pick (see page 39). For milk cartons and other forms of comparable size, it is best to use a large wick because most of these containers are more than 2 inches in diameter.

Homemade Metal Molds. Foremost among these are the regular jello molds found in the kitchen. Candles made from jello molds may be used singly or melted together and stacked one on top of another to form a high candle. Candles made in cupcake molds may also be stacked and inverted. Ordinary tin cans are also suitable as molds, but the top rim must be cut off and the edge

Figure 6: Copper plumbing-tube molds.

must be filed so that the candle can be released without marring the surface.

Metal Plumbing-Tube Molds. Excellent molds can be made of plumber's copper tubing (Figure 6). These tubes are available in many sizes, but you will find those with diameters of 1, 1¼, 1½, and 2 inches to be the most useful. Usually a 10 to 12 inch length is long enough. Be sure the tubes are perfectly straight, with no kinks or bends. Also remember that when tubing is cut, there is generally an overturned edge on the inside; so be sure to remove this edge, using a fine file. Then take a cork that will fit tightly in one end of the tube, put a hole in it for the wick, place it in the tube, and you will have an excellent mold. If you have a wood-turning lathe you can make a combination stopper, base, and formed-candle top all at the same time (Figure 7).

These tube candles are cast, or poured, upside down. See to it that the inside of the copper tubing is highly polished, and use kitchen oil or silicone spray before pouring the wax.

Porcelain and Glass Molds. Use cups, vases, or glasses of any size and shape for molds. Again the only requirement is that they have tapered or slanted sides with no undercuts to impede the release of the candle. Oil the inside for easy release.

If you use a glass mold which is expendable, pour the candle in the usual way and when the wax has hardened, wrap the glass in

Figure 7: Detail of base for copper-tube molds.

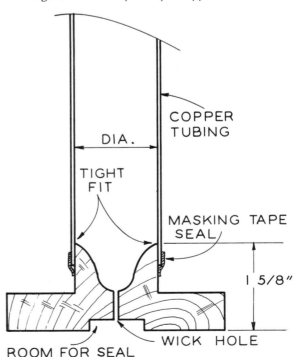

cloth and immerse it in cold water. Then with a hammer, break the outer glass away from the candle. Be careful of sharp pieces of glass when doing this.

Plastic molds. There are two types of plastic molds. The first is the half-mold used in the kitchen for making chocolate and other candy figures; the second is the two-piece mold for casting complete figures.

Both these molds are discussed in greater detail on pages 56–58.

Ceramic molds are very similar to plastic molds; but because they will absorb the hot wax, the inside of the mold should be treated

Figure 8: Representative commercial molds made of tin. Note wick hole in the base.

with *transmission oil*, not regular motor oil. Allow each half of the mold to soak in the oil for several hours, then remove and drain. Another way to prepare a ceramic mold is to give it three or four coats of thinned spar varnish, then two coats of full-strength spar varnish. The varnish spoils the mold for any further plaster casting but is worth it if you have a good shape for a candle. Again, there are a number of manufacturers of fine ceramic molds in hundreds of designs.

Formed paper molds. If you are handy with scissors and paste, you can make any number of individual paper molds of interesting shape and design. Coat the inside of all paper molds with kitchen oil or silicone spray. With care, the same mold can be used several times. (For instructions on making a paper mold, see pages 25–27.

Commercial molds. Candlecrafting has become so popular that a number of firms are now producing metal candle molds in dozens of sizes and shapes (Figure 8). All of these produce professional candles and are used by those who make and sell candles for profit. Most of them are made of polished tin with an attached base that takes the end of the wick. They may be purchased separately, but kits containing complete instructions and all the necessary supplies—candle wax, wick, wick-holding screw and bar, etc.—are also available.

Container molds. These are not true molds in that the finished candle is never removed from the form. Any glass, porcelain cup, or vase may be used. You need not worry about the slanted or tapered sides since the wax remains in the container. A wire-core wick is held in place by means of a metal anchor at the bottom of the mold (Figure 49). These candles make excellent decorative additions to any home and are usually placed on a low table or stand.

Care of Molds

You cannot be too careful with your molds. If they are made of metal, use cleaning or lighter fluid to remove any wax that may adhere to them. If dusty, wash in warm water and cover with cloth bags to keep them clean. It is good practice to clean the mold after each casting so that it will then be ready for the next pouring.

5

Melting and Pouring Wax

Melting Wax

As previously explained, wax should be broken up into small pieces to facilitate and hasten melting. And, again, remember that when melting wax, *always* use a double boiler to eliminate scorching and to prevent the wax from catching fire. If you wish to make your own melting container, you can use—instead of the saucepan setup described on page 16—an iron pot and an oil measuring can of the type used by filling stations (Figure 9). As with the saucepan, a small piece of metal or a trivet should be placed in the water bath to hold the wax container away from the bottom of the pot. By using a wide pot or some other wide water bath, you can melt several cans of differently colored wax at one time, which you will want to do later on.

When using metal molds, heat the wax slowly to about 180 degrees or a little higher. For paper molds and molds other than metal, a temperature of 125 to 135 degrees is advisable. Use your kitchen or candymaking thermometer to check the temperature; but to avoid damaging the thermometer, do not plunge it into wax that is already heated and melted. Instead, place it in the melting pot at the start of the melting; in this way the thermometer heats up at the same rate as the wax.

Figure 9: A convenient and practical setup for melting wax.

Preparing the Mold

The time and energy spent in preparing a mold is usually a good indicator of the success of the finished candle. A poorly prepared mold will produce a poor candle, for the results depend on the mold itself.

COMMERCIAL METAL MOLDS

Before using metal molds, be sure they are thoroughly clean. To remove old wax, pour boiling water over the outside; this will melt the wax inside and allow it to be poured out. Then give the inside surface a light coating of silicone spray.

Next insert the wick into the hole in the bottom of the mold, leav-

Plate 1: Free-form, wax-block candle.

Plate 2: Candles decorated with Swedish decals.

Plate 3: *The interesting texture of this candle was achieved by melting wax of a different color over a plain candle.*

*Plate 4: This sculptured surface, produced with a
hair-curling iron, represents only one of the
seemingly limitless ways to decorate a candle.*

*Plate 5: The strange shapes
formed by a burning
Icelandic candle are
fascinating.*

*Plate 6: The large pine-tree
candle is made with a
mold fashioned from bristol
board; the small one is
molded from a Dixie cup*

Figure 10: Seal the knotted wick securely with floral putty
and masking tape.

ing at least an inch extended. Tie a good-sized knot in this extended
piece of wick, draw it up snugly against the bottom of the mold, and
seal it with floral putty or play clay. (Some of the commercial molds
provide a small screw for the opening in the base, around which the
wick is wrapped and then sealed.) For added protection, cover the
entire bottom opening with masking tape, as shown in Figure 10.
When you are finished with the sealing, pull the wick up to the top

Figure 11: To hold the wick taut, the upper end is tied around
a pencil or stiff wire rod.

of the mold and tie it around a pencil or stiff wire to hold the wick taut (Figure 11).

HOMEMADE CARTON MOLDS

Carton molds are prepared in much the same way as metal molds. The base should be tightly sealed, and the inside of the mold should be given a coating of peanut oil or some other kitchen oil to help release the finished candle. Apply the oil with a swab like the one shown in Figure 2. Make the swab by gluing a piece of cotton to a thin stick—a dowel, for example. The dowel should be at least 14 inches long in order to reach the bottom of deep molds.

The wick may be centered by tying it around a pencil or wire, as explained above. However, if you are using a milk carton, you may find that this arrangement forces the carton into a diamond shape. To hold the carton square, put diagonal strips of masking tape across the corners (Figure 12). When in place, punch a small hole in the exact center of the tapes and thread the wick through. Hold the wick in place with another piece of tape.

Milk-carton molds also have a tendency to bulge out at the sides,

Figure 12: The square shape of a paper-carton mold can be retained by using diagonal strips of masking tape. Note how the wick is held in the center of the mold.

Figure 13: Paper-carton molds are kept square by tying pieces
of thin wood on each side to prevent the sides from bulging.

especially when hot wax is poured into them. Since this bulging
spoils the appearance of the finished candle, it should be prevented
by bolstering the four sides of the carton with pieces of thin paneling
or plywood. Figure 13 shows how to hold them in place with string.
Do not tie the string too tightly, or the sides may cave in. Instead,
apply just enough pressure to hold the sides straight. For a one-quart
carton, cut the supporting pieces 2½ by 7 inches. For a two-quart
carton, the supports should be 3½ by 7 inches. Placing small pieces
of wood across the top of the carton also helps to hold it square.
Though all this preliminary work may seem tedious, it unquestion-
ably results in a better candle.

Heating the Mold

Metal molds should be warm when you pour wax into them or the
candles will not have a smooth finish. One way to heat the mold is
to pour warm water over it, being very careful not to get any water

inside. Another way is to put the mold under a hair dryer or a radiant heat lamp.

To sum up the important points in preparing the mold: make sure it is clean and free of old wax; seal the bottom tightly; have the wick centered and taut; oil the mold for better release; see to it that paper carton molds are square; heat metal molds.

Candle Position

It is usually advisable to cast, or mold, a candle upside down— that is, the top of the finished candle should be at the bottom of the mold. There are two reasons for this. First, if there are any air bubbles in the wax, they will come to the top of the poured wax which will eventually become the bottom of the candle. The top of the finished candle, therefore, will be free of bubbles. Second, as the wax cools, it shrinks, forming a well that must be filled in later with additional wax. It is very difficult to add this wax without producing ring marks; but if they are at the bottom of the candle, they are hidden, and you will have a perfect candle.

Pouring the Wax

When the mold is warm and the wax has reached the correct temperature, begin pouring. With a hot pad or a heavy glove, hold the mold at an angle as in Figure 14 (glove not shown) so that the wax runs down the side of the mold; this prevents splashing and the formation of surface blemishes. Pour the wax to the required level and then place the filled mold in a deep container of warm water. The water should come to not less than 1 inch from the top of the mold. You may have to weight down the filled mold to keep it in place. After making certain that the wick is centered exactly, allow the mold to stand in the water bath for 20 to 30 minutes. This slow cooling allows all air bubbles to rise.

As the wax hardens and shrinks, the deep well or depression, previously referred to, will form at the top of the mold. When a heavy skin forms over the wax and the inside of the candle is still

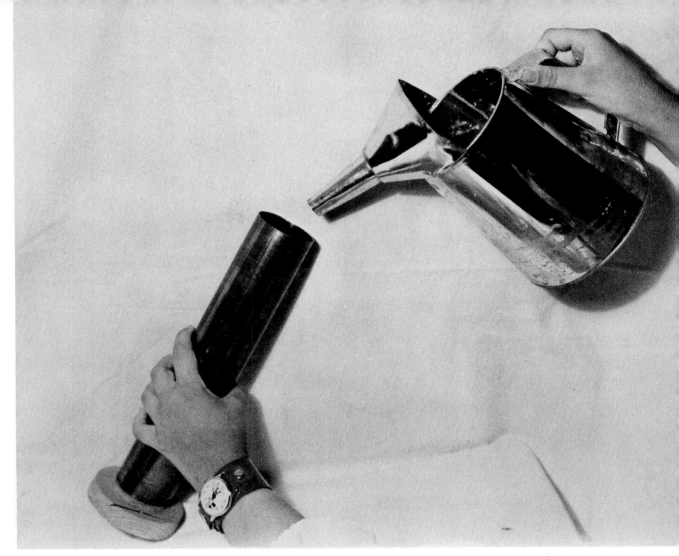

Figure 14: When pouring, tilt the warm mold so that the wax will run along the side of the mold.

liquid, use an ice pick or pencil to punch several holes around the wick as shown in Figure 15. This relieves the interior tension. Remelt the wax that is still in the container and carefully pour some of it into the well. On large candles you may have to do this several times. Be careful not to fill beyond the top of the original pouring; otherwise the new wax may run down between the side of the candle and the mold, thus spoiling the finished candle. The temperature of the wax should be quite high so that it adheres to the candle.

Allow the candle to cool slowly, preferably overnight. Also, if the room temperature is low, cover the mold to keep it from chilling. Always allow plenty of time for cooling because the candle could be ruined if you try to remove it before it is completely set. When the wax is cool and hard, remove the seal at the base of the mold, and give the mold a few light taps. The candle should release easily;

Figure 15: Punching holes around the wick relieves interior tension and keeps the candle from caving in on the sides.

if it doesn't, place the mold in the refrigerator for a little while. If the candle continues to stick after being refrigerated, it means either that you did not use a clean mold, or there is a dent or some other obstruction that keeps the finished candle from dropping out. As a last resort, put the mold under hot water. This will melt the exterior layer of wax and allow the candle to be released. Unfortunately, at the same time, the surface of the candle may be ruined.

The foregoing procedures for releasing candles that stick apply primarily to metal molds. If you are using expendable paper molds, such as milk cartons or orange-juice cans, you can quickly solve the problem of a candle sticking in the mold simply by peeling off the carton.

Whether you use metal or paper molds, you will find a seam line on the side of the finished candle; remove this with a sharp knife. Now check the candle to see if it stands straight. If it doesn't, use the knife to trim the bottom of the candle as much as necessary to correct this fault. Or hold the bottom of the candle on a warm surface so that the wax melts off evenly. The next step, if the candle is *not* to be decorated, is to polish it, using a nylon stocking. If the candle is to be decorated, polish it carefully *after* the decorations have been applied.

Wick Insertion

When you use a cup or glass for a mold, it is impossible to have a hole in the bottom of the unit for the wick; the wick must therefore be added after the candle is poured and hardened. This was done with the dice and snowball candles shown in Figures 30 and 42.

There are two ways of adding the wick. In both instances it is best to soak the wick in melted wax for a few seconds until it is saturated. Before the wax hardens, the wick should be stretched taut. This makes it straight and rigid, and easy to insert in the hole.

One way the wick hole can be made is by heating an ice pick or a piece of coat-hanger wire and then melting a hole all the way through the center of the candle (Figure 16). You will have to reheat the tool several times as you do this. A more efficient way is to drill a hole, as shown in Figure 17, using a ⅛-inch drill. Sometimes a second-hand tool store can supply drills of up to 6 inches in length that you can buy for a few cents. These work very well. The stiffened wick

Figure 16: A hole for the wick is made in a precast candle with a heated ice pick or wire. Note the tool-heating lamp.

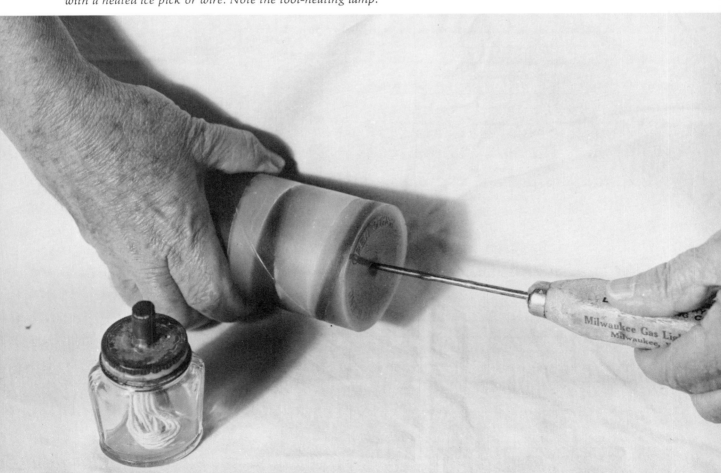

Figure 17: A hole for the wick may be drilled with a ⅛-inch drill.

can be easily inserted (Figure 18) and then sealed in place by means of a heated ice pick or an electric pen.

In some cases, particularly with very special or fancy candles, you need not have the wick run the entire length of the candle. With a heated ice pick, simply make a hole 2 or 3 inches deep at the top of

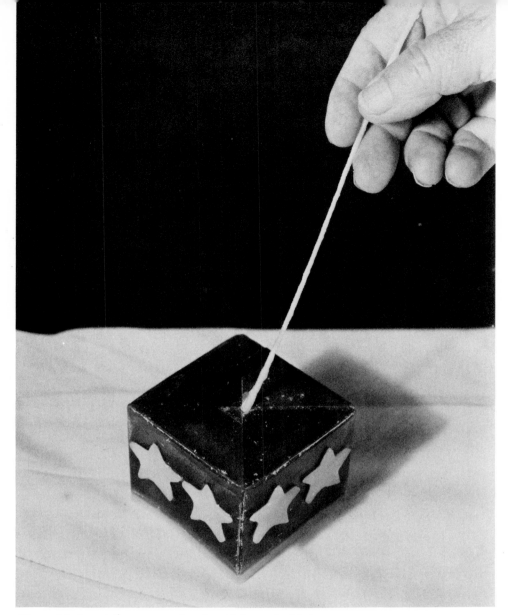

Figure 18: Insert the prewaxed and straightened wick into the hole.

the candle and insert a metal core or waxed wick. As the candle burns down and comes to the end of this wick, repeat the operation with another hole and another short piece of wick.

To preserve a very decorative candle with a large diameter, hollow out the top and insert into the cavity a short second candle to produce the flame. With some candles this cavity is made by burning the original candle. All you have to do in this case is to insert another short wick and refill the hollow with new wax. This procedure will make your original candle last forever.

6

Two Easy-to-Make Candles

To get a general idea of how to make a candle, it is best to start with simple ones, such as those shown in Figures 19 and 20. The directions given will familiarize you with the basic steps for making both a poured and a square candle. To obtain professional-looking results, be sure you have read Chapters 1 through 5 carefully, for these contain information which supplements the following directions. Otherwise your first attempts may produce a poor or mottled surface or some other defect.

Figure 19: These simply made candles were cast by using a deep cup for a mold.

A Poured Candle

For a mold use any deep cup that has slanted or tapered sides, which will make the finished candle release easily. Coat the inside of the cup with a kitchen oil. Melt a sufficient amount of wax in the double boiler and pour it into the cup. When the wax is melted, you may want to color it by adding a few chips of crayon (see page 47).

Let the cup sit for about 6 hours until the wax has set firmly. Then invert the cup and the poured candle will be released. With a heated ice pick or coat-hanger wire, make a hole in the center of the candle for the wick. Using any heavy or medium-size cotton string for the wick, soak it in melted wax, pull it straight as it hardens, and insert it in the hole. Seal the top and bottom of the hole with a bit of melted wax, and your candle is finished (Figure 19).

Figure 20: Paraffin block candle coated with whipped wax.

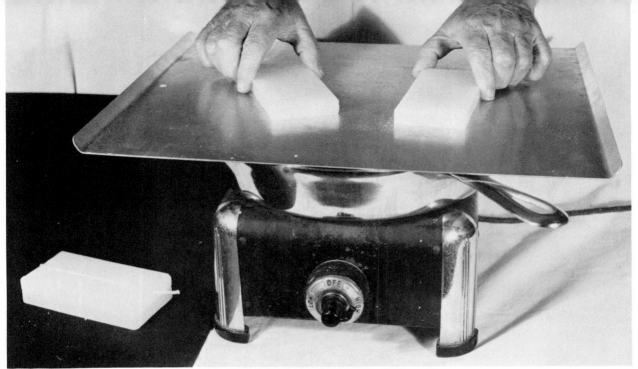

Figure 21: The sides of paraffin slabs are melted so that they may be pressed together to form a larger block.

A Simple Square Candle

A charming and elegant candle (Figure 20) can be made quickly with no extra materials or equipment. Use one box of kitchen paraffin and a piece of heavy white string—the type used to tie heavy parcels. Do not use jute since it will not burn evenly.

Figure 22: Four paraffin slabs melted together to form a candle.

Open the paraffin box and lay out four slabs, or blocks. Put approximately one quart of warm water into an electric frying pan, cover the pan with a cookie tin, and turn up the heat to about 200 degrees. (If you don't have an electric frying pan, place the cookie tin over a pan of boiling water.) In less than a minute the cookie tin will be warm. Hold two pieces of the paraffin flat on the tin (Figure

Figure 23: *Applying whipped wax to the candle's surface.*

21), and soon the sides touching the tin will begin to soften and melt. When they seem quite liquid, quickly press the two pieces together and hold them until the joint solidifies. Repeat this procedure with the other two pieces of paraffin so that you have two half candles. In the center of one of the halves, scratch a groove deep enough to hold the string wick. Hold the wick in place with a bit of melted wax.

Now take the two halves, one with the string side down, and melt the surfaces as you did with the smaller pieces. When the halves seem liquid enough, quickly press them together and hold them until the wax has solidified (Figure 22). If there is any unevenness between the pieces, shave off the high spots with a knife; also square up the bottom.

Next melt one more slab of paraffin in a double boiler and put it in a mixing bowl that has been warmed. As soon as the wax begins to form a skin, take a thin-tined fork or a rotary egg beater and beat the wax into a froth. While the froth is still warm and flexible, spread it over the outside of the candle with a spatula or fork (Figure 23). Allow the froth to harden and you will have a nice square candle with a pleasing snowy, or frothy, surface.

7

Colored Candles

Perhaps the most effective way to make attractive candles is to cast or pour them, using colored wax. There is endless variety in the colors, tints, and shades that can be used.

Colored Crayons

The simplest way to color wax is to use the easily available, ordinary school crayons. Although the crayon method may impair the burning quality of the candle, it does so to such a slight degree that it is of little concern to a beginner. You may want to experiment with leftover bits and stubs of old crayons, but be sure they are the kind that do not have plastic additives (although few of them do).

When your candle wax is melted, pour a small amount into a separate cup or vessel. Shave the crayon into small chips and dissolve them in this wax. Then slowly add this concentrated colored wax to the main wax, stirring constantly to get an even color. Never add the coloring directly to the unmelted main body of wax, for the color will not allow you to see if all of the wax has melted. Adding the color later is the best procedure. As a general rule, one average crayon should be added for each quart of wax, though this will vary since the intensity of the crayon will affect the final color. You can test the color by putting small drops of the wax on white paper; but this test too is sometimes deceiving because the color usually becomes denser and more opaque when the wax has hardened. For close color control, make a small copper-tube candle mold (Figure 6) and cast several small candles, varying the amount of color until you get the right proportion.

The use of stearin, as explained on page 22, will make any colored candle more opaque and thus intensify the color. Stearin should also be used if you want to make pure white candles, although white coloring sticks are also available.

Commercial Colors

Although precolored wax is available from some of the candle supply houses, it is more fun and much more satisfying to mix and produce your own colored wax.

All supply houses have coloring materials that do an excellent job. Most of these are available in small pads, or buttons, of concentrated color. They are used in the same way as the crayons but the colors are more intense. You will also find that when commercial colors are used, your finished candles will burn more evenly, with less smoking and sputtering. Here again you will have to experiment with the amount of color you use in order to get the results you want.

Commercial colors are also available in powdered pigments as well as in liquid dyes, which are very intense. All commercial colors come with complete instructions that are helpful in getting good results.

When you have the proper color, pour the candle as soon as possible. Avoid overheating since it may cause the color to turn a muddy brown. Any colored wax that is left over may be poured into clean tin cans, such as soup cans, and held for future use. You can remelt it later for use in decorating, or in making layered and marbelized candles; or you can mix it all together (which usually produces a brown wax).

Most of the coloring materials come in standard basic colors, although at least one supply house carries candle-coloring buttons, or pads, in fifteen different colors as well as color chips in thirty-six different colors and tints; so it is not necessary to mix your own colors. However, if you prefer mixing your own, here is a handy reference to use as a guide:

To obtain:	Do this:
Black	Use equal parts of red, yellow, and blue.
Brown	Add a small amount of black to orange.
Lavender	Add blue to pink.
Moss green	Add a small amount of red to green (varying amounts of each will make olive and brown)
Orange	Use equal parts of red and yellow.
Pink	Add a small amount of red to white.
Turquoise	Add a small amount of green to blue.

8

Fragrant Candles

A candle is greatly enhanced if the wax emits a fragrance as it burns. A subtle scent adds to the charm and elegance of soft candlelight.

Prescented wax is available from some of the candle supply houses, but you can easily add the fragrance yourself. Do not use ordinary perfumes or colognes, however. These products are unsuitable for candles because they are made with an alcohol base in order to produce rapid evaporation when applied to the skin. Warm wax vaporizes the perfume, and as a result, the alcohol and the scent evaporate. Consquently you will have a nice-smelling place to work in while you're pouring the candles, but no fragrance will be released when the candles are burning.

The proper scent to use has an oil base that is not affected by warm wax. These scents are available from candle supply houses. Use the scent sparingly, however, for too much will become overpowering and ruin the effect. Follow the same rules you use when applying perfume to your person.

There are two ways to scent the wax. Perhaps the best way is to add the scent just before pouring the wax into the mold; this mixes the scent throughout the wax.

The other way is to pour the scent into the tension holes that you punch into the candle while the wax is hardening. Since these holes should be near the wick, the perfume you put in them will not permeate all the wax, but just the inner core.

One supply house lists over twenty different scents, and suggests that ½ ounce (at 75 cents) will scent 4 pounds of wax. Use bayberry for holiday candles; floral scents for dining and living rooms. Adding oil of citronella makes the candle insect-repellent, and thus excellent for patio use.

Figure 24: Free-form candle made from wax blocks.
Also see Plate 1.

9

Candle Shapes
and Decorations

In this chapter a wide variety of candle shapes and designs are illustrated with instructions and suggestions on how to make them. All are basically simple and easy to make. Some are a bit more difficult. Try the simplest first, and then as you become more proficient, make the more complicated ones. In this way, you will avoid disappointment and your skills will improve with each candle you pour and decorate.

Wax-Block Candles

Free-form candles (Figure 24 and Plate 1) are becoming increasingly popular. There is no better way to achieve this free form than to use chunks of wax as they come from the candle supply houses; usually the wax is in slabs about 1½ inches thick.

With an old chisel or screwdriver and hammer, break a wax chunk into pieces of relatively the same size and conformation, such as triangles, squares, or oblongs. Select two pieces that would make an interesting combination, and place the sides to be joined on a warm

Figure 25: Painting hot colored wax on a block candle.

surface—a cookie sheet set atop an electric frying pan (Figure 21) or over a pan of boiling water—to melt the surfaces to an even plane. In one piece, cut a groove and insert a heavy wick, allowing it to extend an inch or more at the top. Then remelt the surfaces and press the two pieces together before the wax has a chance to harden. Hold them firmly until the wax has cooled and the two blocks become one. (If you prefer to add the wick after the two blocks have adhered, do so by drilling or melting a hole [see page 39] for the stiffened wick.) Then place the entire block back on the heated surface to even up the bottom so that the block stands without wobbling. You now have a free-form candle of "modern" design. No two will ever be alike.

For added interest, coat the candle with layers of various colored waxes. Heat small amounts of wax in tin cups or cans and apply it with a small ½-inch brush (Figure 25). You will be surprised at the novel effect this produces. Use earthy colors such as greens, browns, dull oranges, and yellows. Put the darker colors toward the bottom and the lighter colors near the top. Fill the crevices with the darker colors, too. The more colored wax that is dabbed on, the better the result.

Figure 26: Candles decorated with Swedish decals.
Also see Plate 2.

*Figure 27: Two candles cast in two-piece plastic candy molds.
Note how the molds are held together with masking tape,
paper clips, or clothes pins.*

Decorating with Decals

A quick way to decorate candles is to use decals (Figure 26); almost
all hobby shops and home-decorating departments of larger stores
now carry a complete line. Many decals come from Sweden, Norway,
and other foreign countries, and they are extremely well-designed.
Select the decal you want and then plan a candle of appropriate diameter
and height on which to use it. Let the color scheme of the decal
suggest the color for the candle. For most floral designs, harmonizing
colors are recommended (Plate 2). If more modern psychedelic designs
are preferred, the candle color should be intense and vibrant.

Decal decoration is an uncomplicated procedure. Rub the candle
with a nylon stocking to get a smooth, polished surface. Then apply
the decal according to the instructions accompanying it. Usually no
extra precautions need be taken. After the decal is in place, you can,
if you wish, dip the entire candle into the clear wax. This will produce
the illusion that the decal is inside the candle rather than simply applied
to the outside surface.

Plastic-Mold Candles

Many candle supply houses and firms that make molds for ceramic
use also have a line of plastic molds for candymaking. Most of these

Figure 28: Two half-mold figures melted onto a candle molded from a two-quart milk carton.

plastic molds are ideal for candle pouring as well, so long as you remember to keep the wax at a very low temperature in order to avoid damaging the plastic. Candles of almost any shape and description can be made from the hundreds of designs that are available.

Plastic molds, as mentioned earlier, are of two types: two-part and relief. The two-part molds cast a complete figure, whereas the relief molds cast one-half of a figure with a flat back. All two-piece molds can also be used as relief molds. Figure 27 illustrates two two-piece molds—a Santa Claus and a pine tree—as well as the finished candle from each.

To make these figures or similar ones from a two-piece plastic mold, oil the front and back parts, and hold them together with clamps, paper clips, or better still, masking tape. A word of warning here: be extremely careful to see that the molds are sealed as tightly as possible. You may think they are completely sealed, but there may still be an imperceptible gap through which the wax will leak out. When you are satisfied that the two parts are well sealed, pour in the not-too-hot wax .When the wax has cooled, release the candle and add the wick as explained on page 39.

Half-molds can be used by sealing them against a flat surface such as a piece of oiled wood or panel. The relief figure itself is not used as a candle, but is applied to another cast candle, as shown in Figure 28, where the Santa is cast in red wax and the pine tree in deep-green wax. With a heated ice pick or electric wood-burning pen, the figures are melted onto a 4-inch white wax candle poured in a two-quart milk-carton mold. The wick is added later. This candle makes a perfect holiday table decoration. The individual Santas and trees can be used at each place setting for a delightful table arrangement.

Commercial Metal Molds

There seems to be no end to the number, styles, and sizes of the commercial metal molds that are made for pouring candles. One man-

Figure 29: Pyramid candle made from a commercial metal mold.

Figure 30: Dice candles such as this one are made in two-quart milk-carton molds.

ufacturer lists at least fifty different ones in all heights and diameters which are available in circular, square, triangular, starlike, and hexagonal shapes. Figure 29 illustrates the candle produced in a pyramid mold. The candle, 3 inches square at the base and 12 inches high, required 2¾ pounds of deep-blue wax. A heavy, flat, braided wick was used.

Although the candle shown is plain, it is the type that lends itself admirably to formal decoration. Formal floral or geometrically designed paper can be attached with small pins or made to adhere with melted wax. Stylized silver snowflakes also make an attractive pattern, while bands near the top and bottom add more elegance.

In many circumstances a candle with no ornamentation whatsoever is preferable to an elaborate one. If it is well-shaped, correctly proportioned, and attractively colored, no additional decoration is needed, for the candle of itself commands attention.

Dice Candles

The die candle shown in Figure 30 is definitely a conversation piece. It makes a nice gift for use in a family room or for a party, and it is extremely easy to make. Just pour a candle 3¾ inches deep in the

Figure 31: This sculptured white candle was "spanked" with a wire brush to produce a frosted effect.

bottom of a two-quart milk carton. Be sure the carton is "squared up," as explained on pages 34–35, so that the finished candle is a true cube. Use white wax that has been further whitened by the addition of stearin. The heavy wick may be added after the candle is completed. Polish with a nylon stocking.

There are two ways to make the shallow holes for the spots. The easiest way is to heat a melting tool (see page 63) and then to melt in the holes. Another method, the one used for the candle shown, utilizes a round-shaped router bit and a drill press; with these tools you can cut out the holes. In either case, after the holes are in place, take heavy black enamel or dull black paint and paint each indentation. Be sure to place the holes so that those on opposite sides always add up to seven. Study a die for the correct positioning of the spots.

Frosted Sculptured Candle

If for some reason you happen to spoil the outside area of a candle, you can hide your mistake by making the candle shown in Figure 31. The candle itself is made in the usual way. Then, with an ordinary paring knife or a pocketknife, cut rough, irregular, horizontal ridges into the surface. Smooth the ridges and remove all loose wax. Next take an ordinary steel brush with sharp wire bristles and "spank" the candle. The wires will dig into the wax, turning it white, and eventually the whole candle will appear frosted. It is really pretty. White wax is most appropriate for making a candle of this kind.

Melted-Wax-Surface Candles

Today the smooth, highly polished candle surface is no longer in style; instead the rough, natural look is preferred (Figure 32 and Plate 3) and is simple to achieve. The base candle need not have a particularly shiny or smooth surface since all of it will be melted again. Like the frosted candle, the melted-surface candle can be made from a candle whose surface is blemished.

The dark-blue wax candle in Figure 32 is 1½ inches in diameter and 10 inches long. Dark-green wax was melted onto its surface by heating a spatula over a flame and then melting the wax to the candle. If you have an old file on hand (Figure 33), use it instead of the spatula, for it not only holds the heat longer, but allows you to work over

Figure 32: Melted-wax-surface candle.

a larger area and gives you more control over the melting. An alcohol heating lamp is used to heat the applying tool. A candle could be used instead, but it would result in the formation of soot, which might spoil the appearance of the candle.

Figure 33: Making a melted-wax-surface candle with a heated file.

Sculptured Melted-Surface Candles

This method of candle decoration offers yet another opportunity to give free rein to your imagination and ingenuity. These candles (Figure 34), with their geometric designs, are extremely popular and quite simple to make. Pour or cast a candle in the usual way, making it any shape and color you want. As a rule, darker colors lend themselves better to this type of sculpturing. Make a set of "tools" as shown. They can be fashioned from a large-headed nail, a bolt, a hexagon-headed lag screw, a large screw, any small tool that has a square head, etc. Look around the house or your workshop, if you have one, and you will find a dozen or more metal items that will make good tools. Cut a few chunks of wood for handles and fit a handle to each item.

Plan ahead by making a rough sketch of what the finished design should look like. It is often best to use just one or two tool designs per candle, because too many variations may look too "busy" and detract from the overall appearance.

Heat the chosen tool and melt the upper part of the design first (Figure 35). The melted wax will run down the side of the candle but this will melt away as you add further designs on the lower part. Have the tool only hot enough to make two or possibly three impressions. If it is too hot, so much wax will melt that you will have no control over the shapes. Continue until you have covered the entire candle with melted spots. If any wax remains after the last melting, scrape

Figure 34: Sculptured melted-surface candle and the three homemade tools used to create its design.

Plate 7: Striking effects are obtained when decorative materials are embedded in the candle wax.

Plate 8: Eye-catching color combinations enhance these layered candles.

Plate 9: A divided candle is certain to be a conversation piece.

*Plate 10: A simple block candle is given a totally
new look when wax appliqués are added to it.*

Plate 11: Appliquéd candle.

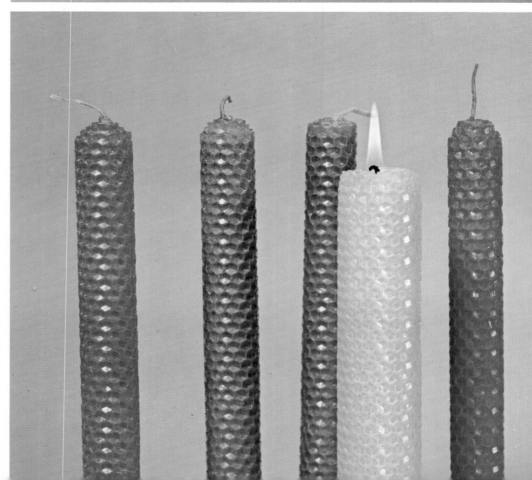

*Plate 12: The beautiful,
natural honeycomb design
of beeswax candles
makes any additional
decoration unnecessary.*

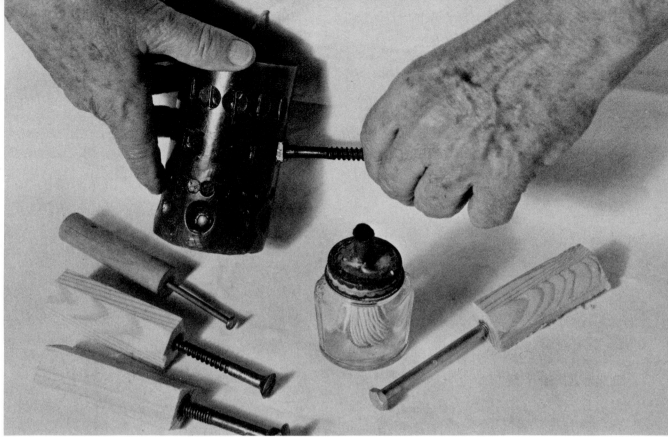

Figure 35: Melting geometric designs into the candle.

it away with a sharp knife. Then polish the entire candle with a nylon stocking.

Sculptured Candles

Perhaps one of the reasons why candlemaking appeals to so many people is that there seems to be no limit to the kinds of decoration that

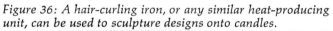
Figure 36: A hair-curling iron, or any similar heat-producing unit, can be used to sculpture designs onto candles.

Figure 37: An artistic sculptured candle.
Also see Plate 4.

can be employed. The dark-blue wax candle in Figure 37 and Plate 4 is an example of this diversity.

After it was poured in the usual way, using a copper-tube mold, the surface was melted with an electric hair-curling iron (Figure 36), which is ideal for this purpose since it does not get too hot and is perfectly safe to use. You can melt grooves, S-curves, dots, dashes, squares, or almost any design you want. The only precaution to take is to have plenty of old papers or cardboard on the floor to catch any dripping wax.

Icelandic Candle

Icelandic candles (Figure 39 and Plate 5) have been produced for a long time and they are fun for the beginner to make because they are really candles within candles.

Using a copper-tube mold and a heavy wick, make the inner candle

Figure 38: Placing small ice cubes around the core candle to make an Icelandic candle.

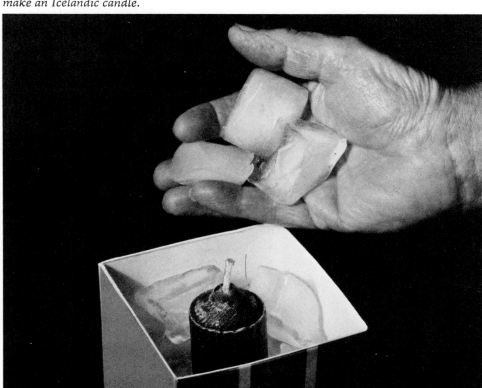

Figure 39: An Icelandic candle with a dark-colored core candle.

in the usual way, about 1 inch in diameter and 7 inches long. Place this candle in the center of a two-quart milk carton. Next melt the wax for the outer candle, having it at the lowest possible temperature at which it will pour nicely. Take small ice cubes, about ¾ inch square, and place them between the inner candle and the mold (Figure 38). (If the ice cubes are too big you will not get an even candle.) Make sure the inner candle is centered; then, as quickly as possible, pour the wax into the mold, filling it to the top of the inner candle. Do not move or disturb during cooling. When the wax has hardened, remove the carton and drain the water from the melted cubes.

The candle is now complete. As it burns it will form various grotesquely intriguing shapes. If the center candle is made of brightly colored wax—the melted wax will run down into the inner open areas and add further interest to the design and appearance.

Figure 40: Greeting-card candle.

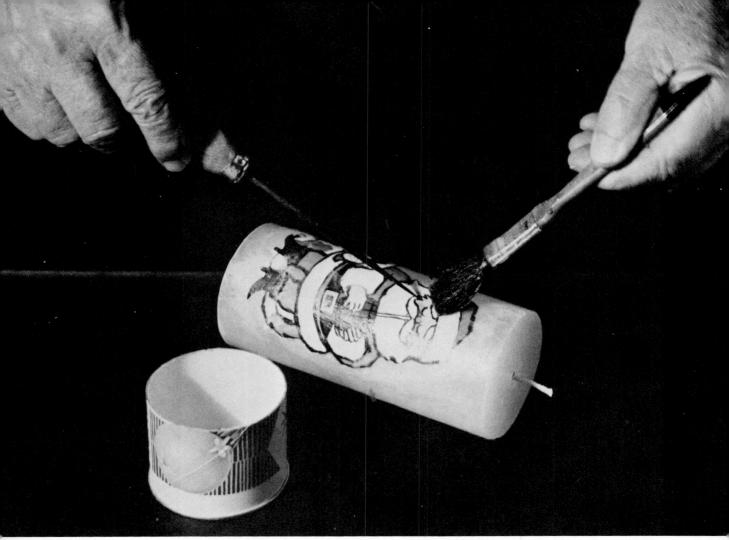

Figure 41: Hold the paper cutout in place with an ice pick and paint on hot, transparent wax.

Greeting-Card Candle

What better way to remember friends and relatives than to put a greeting card they sent you for a special occasion onto a candle? It is a very easy-to-make and thoughtful gift (Figure 40).

Make a candle in the usual way, about 2 to 3 inches in diameter. (White wax is usually best for this project.) Select the card you wish to use. It should have a definite design with a definite outline so that the edges are sharp and clean when it is cut out. It is a good idea, after you've cut out the design, to roll it up, in order to make it curve to the surface of the candle.

Now melt a small amount of clear wax (no stearin), and with a ½-inch brush, wax the design to the candle (Figure 41), starting at one side and proceeding to the other. As you apply the wax, hold the design with an ice pick. Cover the entire surface of the design as well as the surface of the candle with the brushed wax, and the job is finished.

Figure 42: *The popular snowball candle.*

Figure 43: Two half-spheres are cast in a cup for the snowball candle.

It is advisable to burn the candle only until the wax begins to melt at the outside edge of the card design. You can then dig out the center of the candle and replace it with a new short stub. In this way the candle will last practically forever and the design will never be affected.

Snowball Candle

The snowball candle (Figure 42) has always been a great favorite because it is so attractive and yet can be made with so little effort. These candles are extremely popular during the winter season and you can have several in different sizes.

Select a mold such as a tea or coffee cup (Figure 43). It should be as round as possible so that two half-spheres can be cast in it. Oil the mold and pour the two half-spheres. Trim the edges so that the two halves will fit together smoothly, and then melt the edges together, using an electric wood-burning pen or the heated ice pick described on page 85. Next insert a heavy wick, making the hole for it with a heated ice pick.

Finish the candle by covering it with whipped wax (see page 46). If you wish variety, you can cover snowball candles with light tints of yellow, green, or blue wax, although white is recommended for the best effect.

Pine-Tree Candle

These candles (Figure 44 and Plate 6) are ideal decorations for the holiday season. A large amount of wax is required, but after the

*Figure 44: Pine-tree candles.
Also see Plate 6.*

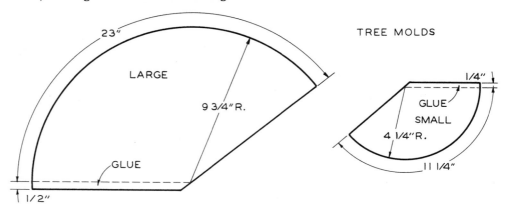

Figure 45: Dimensions for pine-tree molds.

candles have served their purpose the wax can easily be remelted and used for some other candle.

Using heavy bristol board, make cone-shaped molds according to the dimensions given in Figure 45. Seal the seam and be sure it is

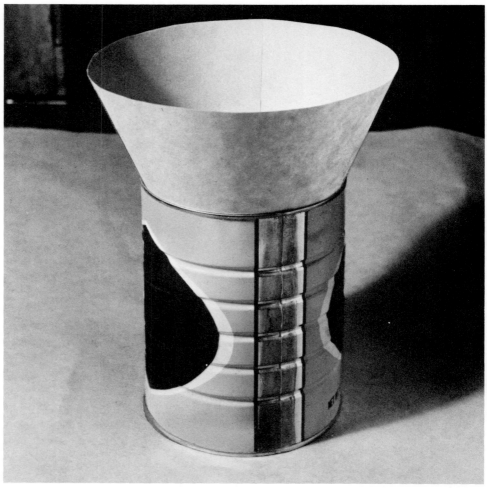

Figure 46: Support tree molds in a suitable container when pouring the wax.

Figure 47: Pillar candle with embedded pine-cone decorations. Also see Plate 7.

Figure 48: Placing pine cones in the space between the core candle and the mold wall.

absolutely tight, since even the smallest opening will cause a messy wax spill. Oil the mold well with peanut oil or some other kitchen oil; then insert it into a suitable can—that is, a can deep enough so that the tip of the mold does not touch the bottom (see Figure 46). Pour dark-green wax slowly into the mold. When it has hardened, release the candle and polish it with a a nylon stocking.

Next whip white wax to which stearin has been added and apply the mixture to the tree candle as shown in Figure 44. Keep the whipped wax at a high temperature so that it will adhere to the tree. Finally, drill a hole in the top and add a large-size wick.

The procedure for making the small tree also seen in Figure 44 is the same, except that Dixie cups can be used for the molds. For a festive holiday table, use the large tree for a centerpiece and arrange the small ones at each place setting.

Candles with Embedded Decorations

Infinite variety is possible when you decorate candles with embedded materials. As you can see from Figure 47 and Plate 7, small pine cones are enclosed within the wax, yet they remain visible.

To make a candle like this, use a copper-tube mold to pour a candle 1 inch in diameter, with a large wick. Place this core candle in a mold with a 3 inch diameter, centering it carefully and holding it in place at the bottom with a small amount of wax. Then, as shown in Figure 48, insert the cones in the space between the core candle and the mold wall, and position them correctly with a thin dowel or a stick. The candle is more attractive if the cones are kept toward the bottom, as are the ones shown in the illustration. When all the cones are in position, fill the mold with candle wax. This wax should not contain any stearin, for, as you'll recall, stearin makes wax opaque and the cones therefore would not be seen.

For a candle of this kind, almost any article may be substituted for the cones. Try such items as marbles, artificial flowers, corn, seeds, fruit pits, acorns, etc. Another variation is to make small wax cubes of various colors and place them around the center candle. If you try this idea, keep the temperature of the wax poured into the mold at the lowest possible point so that it does not melt the wax cubes.

When using artificial flowers, attach them to the small inner candle first and then lower the entire candle into place. In this way the spacing and arrangement of the flowers will be more attractive than if they were put in place from above with the dowel or stick. After you have made just one candle like this, you will be anxious to try many variations.

Three-Wick Candle

A low three-wick candle, like the one in Figure 49, is a handsome accessory for a cocktail table and takes scarcely any time at all to make. An ordinary cheese-dip carton was used to make the candle illustrated. The wick, however, is special. A small-size metal-core wick is fastened to a metal anchor available from a candle supply house. The metal core holds the wick upright. Three of these are placed in the oiled mold and the wax is poured in as usual. As the wax hardens, the wick can be correctly spaced and placed.

Although metal-core wicks work best, if they are not available you can use regular wicking tied to small buttons, which will serve as anchors to hold them in place. Suspend the wicks from above by attaching them to a cut-down carton, or arrange some other device that will hold the wicks upright.

Layered Candles

To make layered candles successfully, an extra ingredient is necessary—patience. You cannot hurry the process and have a nice candle. Twelve-ounce orange-juice paper containers were used for the candles illustrated in Figure 50 and Plate 8. One candle was set upright while the other was set at a slant, balanced on a small wooden block (Figure 51). Deep brown, orange, and yellow wax was used.

Melt each color in a large tin can on which you have formed a spout by pinching the top rim on one side. Pour a layer of the melted wax into each oiled mold and allow it to cool and harden almost completely before pouring the next layer. In this process, timing is most important. If the first layer of wax is too hot, the second layer will mix with it and both will be ruined. On the other hand, if the first layer is too hard, it may be difficult to get the second layer to adhere to it. Just watch closely and you will be able to tell when the wax should be poured. If the slanted mold is rotated from layer to layer you will not only get layers but triangles of various colors, as shown in Figure 50 and Plate 8. Also keep the wax at the lowest possible temperature so that it will not melt the wax already in the mold.

Figure 49: A simple three-wick candle that was molded from a cheese-dip carton. Note the wire-core wick on an anchor.

Figure 50: Layered candles in which horizontal and triangular
layers have been produced.

Try various color combinations: red, white, and blue; dark green,
blue, and white; black, coral, and red—any colors that you wish.
Keep in mind, too, that this is a handy and attractive way to use up
wax left over from other candles. If you use a large water bath (see
page 18), you will be able to keep several cans of wax melted at the
same time. Set the heat at the lowest possible level to keep the wax
ready for each layer and at the correct low temperature.

Figure 51: Layered candles are molded from 12-ounce
orange-juice cans. To create slanted color bands, tilt the mold.

Figure 52: Divided candle.

These layered candles are poured without a wick. The wick is inserted later by drilling a hole or melting a hole with a heated ice pick (see page 39).

Divided Candle

A divided candle is a very novel item and a conversation piece wherever it is used. The candle in Figure 52 and Plate 9 was poured upside down, using a cake-mix box as a mold. A small wooden box form was glued to the sides and bottom of the cardboard box, making a wax-tight seal (Figure 53), and the cardboard form was heavily oiled for easy release.

The candle shown is 5½ inches wide, 5½ inches high, and 1⅜ inches thick, with upright candles that are 2¾ inches high. The wicks were added after the candle was poured. The appliquéd design is 1⅜ inches by 4 inches and ⅛ inch thick. The three square holes were melted through with a square melting "tool" after the appliqué had been applied to the candle.

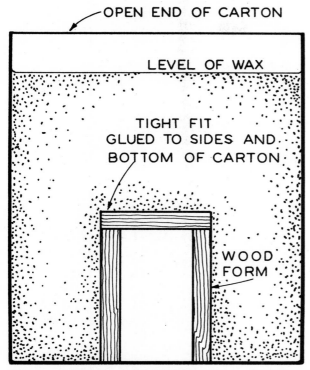

Figure 53: Side view of the mold used for a divided candle. Note the wooden form attached to the sides and bottom of the mold.

This same procedure could be used for making a candle with three uprights.

Appliquéd Candles

Years ago candle decoration included appliquéd wax designs in the form of flowers and leaves made of thin wax. Although these forms are still popular to some extent, today's applied designs are more often geometric in shape. Appliquéd candles require a little more time and work to produce, but the results more than justify the effort you put into them (Figures 54 and 55). Begin by making a candle of any shape and color you want. Then make the wax sheet for the appliqués as follows.

First decide what color wax you will use for the appliqués. (The candle shown in Figure 54 and Plate 10 is deep coral with dark-brown appliqués.) Place a cookie tin over a skillet or frying pan filled with water on your heating plate. On top of the cookie tin, place an

Figure 54: Block candle with appliquéd geometrical designs.
Also see Plate 10.

Figure 55: Stylized flower designs appliquéd to a tube candle.

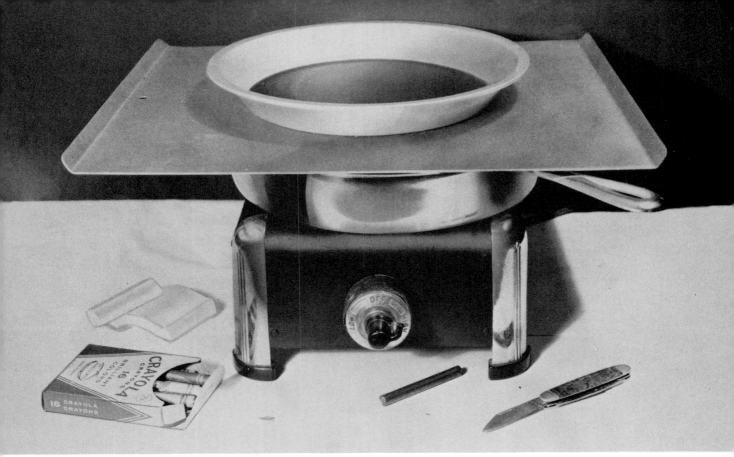

Figure 56: Setup for melting a wax sheet.

aluminum plate or a pie tin in which to melt the colored wax (Figure 56). Melt enough wax to make a layer ⅛ inch thick.

When the wax is melted, lay the pie tin on an absolutely level surface. As soon as the wax begins to set, cut out the design parts (Figure 57) with small play cookie cutters, a glass, a can with a sharp edge, or any other suitable form. You can also cut the pieces freehand into stylized leaf, flower, and stem shapes, as was done for the candle

Figure 57: Wax sheet cutouts.

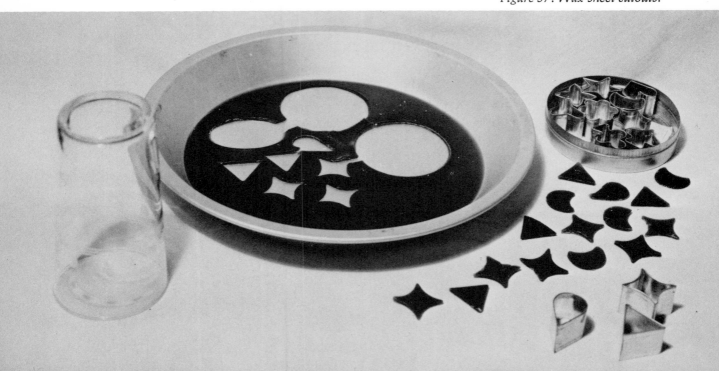

Figure 58: Place wax cutouts in a dish of hot water to keep
them pliable.

in Figure 55. Whether you use a form or work freehand, the shapes
for the appliqués must be cut while the wax is still pliable. You will
find that they begin to harden in a few minutes, but don't be con-
cerned about this. Merely place the cutouts in a bowl of hot water
(Figure 58) and they will start to soften; you can then take your time
applying them to the candle.

Lay the candle on its side, and position the cutouts on it in what-
ever arrangement you wish. Next make an adhering tool from an ice
pick by rounding off the tip so that it is wide and blunt (Figure 59).
If you wrap some wire around the tool, it will help to retain the heat,
thus enabling you to apply several appliqués with each heating. The
small alcohol heating lamp described on page 18 is handiest for heating the tool, although a candle can be used instead; it will, however,
become sooty, as was pointed out previously.

To apply the design piece, hold it in place with another ice pick
(Figure 60), heat the tool, and run the blunted tip around the edges of
the appliqué; this will melt the piece to the candle. It is as simple as
that. After applying just one or two pieces, you will become very
adept at making a fine thin edge of melted wax.

Once the appliqué pieces have been cut from the wax sheet and re-
heated, they may be further shaped or embossed with any appro-

Figure 59: A soft wire wrapped around a blunted ice pick
will help the tool retain heat.

BLUNT, ROUND POINT

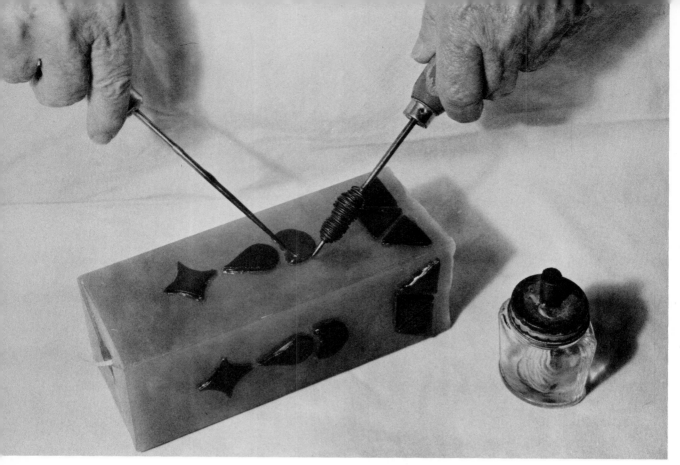

Figure 60: Appliqué designs are held in place with an ice pick and melted to the candle.

priate device. Figure 61 shows a circular piece that was first cut out of the wax sheet with a drinking glass. When softened, it was perforated with a glass insulator that had "raindrops" along its lower

Figure 61: After they have been cut out of the wax sheet, appliqué pieces can be further shaped and embossed with suitable forms.

edge. The oval piece in the same illustration was made by means of a glass salt cellar with an embossed bottom. Just a casual look around your home will turn up any number of glass and porcelain items that can be used to form and shape intricate designs on appliquéd wax sheets and pieces.

Additional Appliqué Designs

Figure 62 and Plate 11 provide an example of pieces appliquéd to a candle by yet another procedure than the one just described. The main candle body was made of deep-yellow wax poured into a two-quart milk-carton mold. The round piece of dark-brown sheet wax on the right side of the candle was made in the customary way. But the unit on the left side was made by pouring the wax into a well-oiled glass dish that had a hunting scene with a horse and rider embossed in the bottom. Both circular designs were then adhered to the candle as described above. You may have dishes, ashtrays, or other glass pieces that can be used to make equally attractive appliqués.

Figure 62: Candle decorated with appliqués made by two different processes.

10

Rolled Beeswax Candles

Beeswax candles (Figure 63 and Plate 12) are ideal in many ways. They burn evenly without sputter or smoke; they have a subtle, enticing odor of honey; and, they are very, very easy to make. You need no equipment whatsoever. All that is necessary is a sheet of beeswax and a wick.

Beeswax usually comes in 8 by 16½ inch sheets, enough to make two candles. Candle supply houses carry beeswax especially made for candles in at least 17 different colors, so you can make candles to fit any color scheme you have in mind.

Cut the beeswax sheet in half lengthwise, so that it measures 8 by 8¼ inches. Then cut a square-braided or a "fine" wick about 9½ inches long. To facilitate even and simple rolling, first place the beeswax sheet on a cookie tin over a pan or skillet of lukewarm water (Figure 64). Since beeswax melts quickly, it is important to watch the temperature carefully. Place a ruler or some other straightedge about ¼ inch from the edge of the wax sheet, and with the ruler as a guide to keep the sheet straight, turn the wax up to form a groove for the wick. Slip the wick in the groove, fold the wax over it, and then carefully begin rolling the wax, keeping it even and straight. After one or two turns, the candle will seem to straighten by itself. Continue until the wax is all rolled up. On the last turn, carefully press down the edge of the wax sheet so that it melts onto the body of the candle, and the candle is completed.

Figure 63: Rolled beeswax candle.

For a final touch, trim the top edge of the wax at a slant away from the wick (see Plate 12). This will taper the top of the candle and add to its appearance. However, do not trim more than ⅜ inch off the sheet.

Figure 64: A sheet of beeswax is rolled on a cookie sheet over a skillet of warm water.

11

Helpful Hints
and Solutions
to Common Problems

Frost Marks

Though frost marks may be caused by pouring the wax into a mold that is too cold or by forcing the candle out of the mold before it is completely cooled, the usual reason for them is that the wax was not hot enough when it was poured. Frost marks can be polished away by rubbing the candle briskly with a soft cloth or a nylon stocking.

Pit Marks

Wax that is too cold when poured will create air bubbles that become trapped inside the candle; these air bubbles, in turn, cause pit marks. To avoid them, make sure the wax is heated to about 175 degrees; this temperature will allow the bubbles to rise and escape.

Pit marks may also be caused by pouring the wax too quickly or by the presence of lint and dust in the mold. Therefore pour the wax slowly, and see that the mold is clean and polished.

90

Internal Fracture Marks

Internal fracture marks result from cooling the candle too rapidly. Control the cooling by leaving the poured candle in its mold and submerging the whole unit in warm water for about a half hour. This not only ensures slower cooling and fewer fracture marks, but it also allows trapped air bubbles to rise and escape.

Mottled Appearance

There may be several reasons for this defect: the candle may have cooled too slowly if it is summertime or if the room is too hot. Or the wax used may have been too old and remelted too many times. In most cases, however, a mottled appearance results from a lack of stearin.

Shiny and Pitted Candles

If candles are shiny and pitted, chances are the wax was too hot when poured. Although wax does not boil, any moisture in it will boil at 212 degrees, forming bubbles of steam that become trapped. Pour the wax at 175 degrees for the best results.

Seams and Blemishes

The joining seam in a metal mold leaves a ridge on the candle which can be removed with a knife or spatula. Hold the knife at right angles to the candle and slide it down the seam. Pull firmly without any vibration which could leave a chatter mark. When the surface is smooth, polish the candle with a nylon stocking.

Caved-in Candles

Sometimes you may find that a candle has caved in at the middle. This is the result of neglecting to poke vent holes in the partially set candle. These vent holes are necessary to relieve the stress of the shrinking wax and to eliminate the vacuum which causes cave-ins.

Releasing Difficulties

If you used inferior wax, you may encounter difficulties in releasing a candle from its mold. It is more likely, however, that the sides of the mold had dents or other convex areas which gripped the candle and thus impeded its release. This problem may also be caused, after the poured candle has set, by wax that has run down between the candle and the wall of the mold; so when filling in the depression in the base of the candle, be sure that no wax runs down the side.

If none of the above seem to be creating the problem, yet the candle sticks even though the mold feels cold, place the mold in the refrigerator for an hour, and then try again. This additional cooling may make the candle contract just enough to effect release. If this still doesn't work, then the only way to get the candle out is to pour hot water on the outside of the mold. This will ruin the finish of the candle, but at least it will be out of the mold.

Under no circumstances should you ever pry the candle loose; if you do, the upper edge of the mold may be dented and ruined.

Excessive Smoking and Dripping Wax

If the candle smokes continuously, in all likelihood it is because the wick is too big.

If the wax drips, either the wick is too small or the wax did not have enough stearin in it.

Adding Color

Be sure all the wax is melted and in liquid form before you add color chips or colored melted wax to it. If the color is added prematurely, it will be difficult to see whether or not the wax has completely melted because you will not be able to see the bottom of the melting pot. If any of the wax remains solid when the candle is poured, chunks of uncolored wax will show up as defects in the finished candle, thereby ruining it.

Melting

Although the precautions to be taken when melting wax have been discussed previously, they are so important that they bear repeating: (1) never, never melt wax over an open flame; always melt it over a water bath such as a double boiler; (2) high temperatures are not needed in making candles—175 degrees is just about right under all conditions; In any case, never go beyond 200 degrees; (3) never leave melting wax unattended, and be sure to keep children away from it; (4) have plenty of newspapers or old flattened cartons on the table and floor in the working area; wax has a way of spilling even when extreme care is taken to prevent it.

One additional word: never pour melted wax down the sink, for it will most certainly clog the drain.

Suppliers

If you live in a fairly large city, you doubtless will be able to obtain all your candle supplies at local hobby dealers or crafts supply houses. You will find them listed in the Yellow Pages of the telephone directory. (Also see page 21.)

American Handicrafts Co.
1001 Foch Street
Fort Worth, Texas 76107

Bersted's
Box 40
Monmouth, Illinois 61426

California Artificial Flower Co.
400 Reservoir Avenue
Providence, Rhode Island 02907

The Candle Mill
East Arlington, Vermont 05252

Duncan Ceramic Products, Inc.
5673 E. Shields Avenue
Fresno, California 93727

General Supplies Co.
Box 338
Fallbrook, California 92028

General Wax and Candle Co.
6858 Beck Avenue
North Hollywood, California 92647

The Glow Candle Co.
Box 10102
Kansas City, Missouri 64111

Lee Ward's
840 N. State Street
Elgin, Illinois 60121

Maid of Scandinavia Co.
3245 Raleigh Avenue
Minneapolis, Minnesota 55416

Murray's
Box 578
San Marcos, California 92069

Pourette Mfg. Co.
6818 Roosevelt Way N. E.
Seattle, Washington 98115

A. I. Root Co.
Medina, Ohio 44256

Frank B. Ross Co., Inc. (Waxes only)
6–10 Ash Street
Jersey City, New Jersey 07304

W. Wooley & Co.
Box 29
Peoria, Illinois 61601

Index